MW00412154

CHANGE THE WORLD

Make Big Money Teaching, Training & Serving Humanity

By the 2-Time #1 Best-Selling Author
CHRISTIAN MICKELSEN

Copyright © 2012 Christian Mickelsen. All rights reserved.

No portion of this book may be reproduced mechanically, electronically, or by any other means, including photocopying, without written permission of the publisher. It is illegal to copy this book, post it to a website, or distribute it by any other means without permission from the publisher.

Christian Mickelsen

Christian@CoachesWithClients.com

619-320-8185

San Diego, CA

Limits of Liability and Disclaimer of Warranty

The author and publisher shall not be liable for your misuse of this material. This book is strictly for informational and educational purposes.

Warning – Disclaimer

The purpose of this book is to educate and entertain. The author and/or publisher do not guarantee that anyone following these techniques, suggestions, tips, ideas, or strategies will become successful. The author and/or publisher shall have neither liability nor responsibility to anyone with respect to any loss or damage caused, or alleged to be caused, directly or indirectly, by the information contained in this book.

ISBN-13: 978-1490997063

ISBN-10: 1490997067

Contents

R

CHAPTER 1

Wanted: A Few Daring Souls For an Adventure of a Lifetime...

I was outraged, frustrated, and upset when I saw these "internet marketers" making tens of thousands, hundreds of thousands, even millions of dollars selling online training programs.

It wasn't fair that these uncaring, cold-hearted, money grubbing bastards were making so much money while I, a big hearted, super caring, heart-centered success coach who had so much to share with the world was only making around $40K/year.

But then I got inspired.

I thought, if they can make all this money doing something that I love to do - teach, train, and inspire - then I should be able to do it too. I'd just have to figure out how to do it authentically (and not be all slimy like they are).

I set out to create my first "information product". I set a modest goal to make $100,000. I spent weeks creating my first program.

And I sold nothing. $0, nada, nothing, zip, zilch.

I felt rejected by the world. I felt like a failure and a loser. I almost gave up. The only things that spurred me on were the urge I had inside me to share the lessons I'd learned in my life, and the promise of making more money than I've ever made in my lifetime (plus, I couldn't let those sneaky marketers beat me).

Over the next few years I studied everything I could get my hands on to learn how to create the trainings that people really wanted, and how to explain the value of what was in those programs so they would see the value and invest in them.

I also had to overcome a lot of my own personal character flaws. Things like fear of rejection, perfectionism, arrogance, fear of failure, and fear of success. Let me tell you, I was a mess.

But it was worth it. I've sold millions of dollars of training programs over the years and this has changed my life in so many ways. I learned that I could have anything I wanted, if I put my mind to it.

I met and married my dream girl (we now have 2 kids). I moved to my dream city: San Diego. I've made Hawaii my second home (in fact I'm writing this in Hawaii right now). I get to drive around in fancy cars. I get to provide a great life for myself and for my family.

All of this is great, but the thing I love the most is getting emails and Facebook comments from people whose lives are changing because of my programs. Seriously, watching people have huge breakthroughs and total life transformations because of what I've shared with them is absolutely priceless.

"Beating the slimy marketers" isn't really important to me any more. Honestly, I've gotten to know a lot of those guys over the years and I came to realize that they aren't really bad guys. They were just pushing a little too hard to make money. Most of them actually wanted to help people too - just like me. Of course there are some truly slimy guys (and gals) out there, but they make up less than 10% of the folks out there.

One other thing you might be interested to know is that while I've made millions, I've also invested hundreds of thousands in training and coaching for myself. I needed to learn a lot and I needed to overcome a lot of my own "stuff" in order to get where I am today. It wasn't easy.

It was the hardest thing I've ever had to do. It wasn't hard like shoveling concrete, or delivering king size mattresses up 3 flights of stairs all by myself (jobs I had as a young man). It was hard in a different way. It pushed a lot of my buttons. I had to take many leaps of faith. And in the end, if I had known how hard it was going to be when I first started, I probably never would have gone for it.

But it was worth all of the tests, challenges, and failures to be able to live my life on my own terms, and watch as the world changes because of what I'm teaching.

CHAPTER 2
My Character Flaws

I'm not perfect. No one is. Or maybe we all are perfect just as we are. Nonetheless, I'm still working on myself.

I'm still working on letting go of my insecurities, self-judgments, and limiting beliefs.

Here are some of the character flaws I have had to overcome to achieve the success I have with selling online training and coaching programs. I'm telling you this so that you understand that I'm just a regular guy and if I can create huge success, you can too.

Laziness

I really hated myself for being lazy. There were certain things I liked do and certain things I hated doing. I wanted someone else to do the things I didn't like to do, but I saw other people that could do everything themselves and I was mad at myself because I couldn't or wouldn't.

My breakthrough came not from overcoming my laziness, but from accepting it.

OK, there are certain things I just stink at and I don't enjoy at all. The great thing is, there are other people that are good at them and enjoy them. I started hiring people to help me. First I found a part time virtual assistant that could do a lot of the technical stuff (handling websites, shopping carts, etc.).

Over the last several years I've built an awesome team of people that do the stuff they're great at (that I'm not) and they love doing, so I can just show up and do the things I enjoy.

Fear of Rejection

I used to be so afraid that people wouldn't like my ideas. I remember when I would ask people for feedback, sometimes I would say, "just tell me what you like about it" because I didn't want to hear anything negative.

The problem is that you can't really make things better without hearing both the good and the "needs improvement".

I'm not sure where my fear of rejection came from; maybe from being teased as a kid; maybe from teachers marking up my papers. Who knows? Ultimately it doesn't matter where these things come from as long as they go away.

Arrogance

I thought I knew it all. I knew what people needed to learn so I created the programs that I "knew" they needed. Then I tried to sell them. Then I was really frustrated when people didn't buy them. Arrrgggghhh!!!! What was I doing wrong?

I realized that I didn't know what people needed to learn. Or more accurately, I didn't know what they WANTED to learn. So I started asking folks things like: "What do you most want to learn about _____?" and, "What's the biggest challenge you're facing with _____?" Then they would tell me exactly what they wanted and what they felt like they needed.

Wow. It was crazy, but when I started creating programs that taught people what they already told me they wanted, they started selling!

I also realized that they did need the things I originally thought they needed to learn. They just didn't know they needed it. So I snuck it into the programs without them realizing it. It's like putting vitamins in a chocolate bar. They need the vitamins but they want the chocolate.

I was also arrogant in thinking I could figure out how to make lots of money and change the world selling online training programs all by myself. I failed a lot on my own. But once I started studying lots of other gurus that had already tried and tested and proven certain principles, that's when things really took off for me.

I had to swallow my pride and admit that I still had a lot more to learn.

Perfectionism

Most people don't know this but I still struggle with perfectionism at times. I've been working on a book that's very near and dear to my heart for nearly 3 years. But I haven't released it.

Why? Because I don't want people to not love it. (Wow, that was hard to admit to myself).

On the other hand, I've created over 30 different online training and coaching programs over the last 8 years, and all of them have flaws. The audio and video quality isn't perfect all the time. I say "um" and "ah" a lot (much to the dismay of my speech teacher and my fellow Toastmasters). There are typos.

One of my best friends shared something with me years ago:

"Done is better than perfect."

I realized that I'd never make money or help anyone if I kept working on something until it was perfect - because there is no such thing as perfect. And when I looked inside deep enough I could see that my perfectionism was really just fear of failure or fear of rejection (or both).

Fear of Success

When I first heard of this fear, I thought it was ridiculous. Why would anyone fear success? That's just crazy. But, then I experienced it - over and over.

The first time was when I created my first hit program. I started making around $25K/month and it was really uncomfortable. Keep in mind that the most money I'd ever made from a regular job was $35K/year and I was raised by a single mom working as a waitress with 4 kids. We grew up on food stamps and special lunch programs. I wore hand-me-down clothes from brothers that were 8 and 9 years older than me. Bell-bottom jeans just weren't cool anymore in the 80's and I got teased a lot.

So I had a lot of weird thoughts and feelings come up when I started making what felt like "crazy money" at the time:

- Rich people are bad (uh oh, I'm getting rich).

- My "poor" family is going to want me to give them all of my money.

- Who am I anyway? Why do I deserve to make all this money?

- Money isn't fair. Why should some people suffer financially while others do well?

- People who make lots of money should give it all away.

- Money is the root of all evil.

It's a wonder how anyone gets rich or successful with these kinds of thoughts and feelings inside. And you know what, probably no one does - at least not for long. Guess what I did?

Yep, after really crushing it for a while in a program that people loved, I ended the program and went on to other "new and exciting" projects. Basically I kept re-inventing things and didn't let my income grow any higher for a couple of years.

Then I realized I really wasn't serving humanity to the best of my ability by "playing small".

I decided to step up and be a leader in this world and I worked through tons of my "stuff" around money and success. Since then I've watched my income soar from $40K/year as a success coach, to over $100K/year, to $250K/year, to $500K/year, to $750K/year, to $1M/year and more.

I now know that money is a good thing. It's given me the freedom to work just 20 hours/week and spend lots of quality time with my wife and my little girls. It's given me the resources to take great care of my health and my family's health. It's let me contribute to the world through charities.

Rich people are good and bad just like everyone else.

Money isn't fair, but that's OK. Life is great even when things aren't fair.

People who "suffer financially" have opportunities to improve their situation. It's up to them to take them (just as I did).

If my family wants me to give them all of my money, I can just say "no", or I can give them some if I want to—it's really up to me and I don't need to be afraid of people asking me for help.

Money isn't evil. Making money by hurting, cheating, or stealing from others is evil. Money itself is a life-enhancing, fun, and helpful tool.

How I Overcame My Character Flaws

Over the years I've studied like crazy on how to overcome my fears, insecurities, and limiting thinking. I've read lots of books (at one point I read 36 books in 36 weeks). I've been trained in powerful techniques such as NLP and hypnotherapy. I've gone to seminars with lots of personal growth gurus (Like Tony Robbins, Byron Katie, Deepak Chopra, Wayne Dyer, Don Miguel Ruiz, and Dan Millman, to name a few).

Eventually, I created my own techniques for working through this stuff faster than anything I could find from any of these amazing teachers. I'll share one of my favorite techniques with you at the end of this book (it's called "The Peace Process"). If you're in the same position I was in and want more support, reach out to me to work 1-1 with me personally or with one of the hand picked, personally trained coaches on my team.

Also, I want you to keep in mind that I'm not perfect and that I still have "character flaws" and that as humans we always will. But in fact, they really aren't flaws. They are just challenges on our journey. New challenges and new journeys bring up new insights about ourselves that we can learn from and grow through.

CHAPTER 3
The Weird Dynamic of Getting Paid to Help People

NOTE: Skip this chapter if you never feel any hang-ups around charging money to help people. Everyone else, keep reading.

Somehow folks that love helping people, like myself, get it into their minds that they shouldn't charge a lot of money to help people. I think deep down, we see folks suffering and we want to end their pain and sometimes charging money just feels wrong.

In order for anyone to sell anything, what's being sold HAS to help people. Think about it. Your car helps you get around. Your home gives you shelter. Your clothes keep you warm. And…

Your car, home, and clothes can make you feel cool, fun, sexy, playful, and powerful. These are all life-enhancing experiences. They bring joy to our lives.

But what if someone is hungry. Is it wrong to charge someone for food? Obviously not! Grocery stores and restaurants do it every day. Is it wrong to charge a sick person for medicine? People buy aspirin and cold remedies every day.

If people are in pain, we as coaches, healers, helpers, teachers, and trainers *really* want to help them. And they really want our help. So what's wrong with letting folks pay for our help? Nothing. But…

If you still have feelings that somehow we shouldn't charge for the work we do, then keep the following ideas in mind.

Powerful Truths About People & Money

1. People are 100% whole, complete, and capable of amazing things (people are not weak, needy, and helpless). People can choose to get your help, or not. They are on their own path and working with you right now might be perfect for them or it might not be perfect now, or ever.

2. People buy what's important to them—even if it doesn't make sense to us (people might pay for their cable bill before they pay their health insurance, or say they can't afford to get acupuncture, but go out and buy a bunch of new clothes).

3. If you market the way I teach marketing, you'll be helping folks with powerful advice and training that you share for free. You can help hundreds, thousands, tens of thousands, hundreds of thousands, or even millions of people for free. And the more folks you help for free, the more folks will pay to learn more from you.

4. No matter how much you charge, there will be people that can't afford it. And the opposite is also true. No matter how much you charge, there will be people that CAN afford it.

5. I've had great clients and students that have paid me lower amounts of money. But, most of my best clients and students tend to be the ones that invest the most. They're committed to results and willing to pay for the help they need to get them.

6. Simply paying for coaching and training starts the change. As soon as someone pays you they're already much further down the path of success than they were one minute ago. Some folks will start getting results before they even listen to the first lesson, just from the energy and enthusiasm they get from making the decision to join your programs.

Bottom line: Let people pay you for what you have to offer. Your programs are a gift to this world. You deserve to be well paid for what you contribute.

CHAPTER 4
If I Can Do It, So Can You

I want to tell you how to help a lot of people and make a lot of money with your teaching, training, and coaching services. Let me tell you more about this dream of information (info) products and the journey that I took to get to where I am today.

I first heard of info products and online training programs 14 or 15 years ago—pretty early on in the Internet days. The Internet is always changing and evolving, but as a viable economic format, it's really only been around for 15 years or less. It's such an integral part of our lives, that's hard to imagine!

I signed up and purchased online training programs myself and learned a bunch of stuff from them. Usually they were lower priced programs in the early days (often under $200). I also purchased live event passes, and I used to go to seminars online.

Then I started seeing people selling a lot of stuff online, and I started thinking, "Wow, that sounds great." Then people started selling "how to make money selling stuff online" kind of programs, and I started seeing the numbers those people would talk about.

As I mentioned earlier, I saw people making tens of thousands of dollars; hundreds of thousands of dollars; even making millions of dollars. I thought, "Whoa, that's pretty crazy." I was a little skeptical, but if people are really doing that, then that's really great.

Then I got hired by someone, whose name I will keep anonymous, and he was selling information programs to his list. I was watching him.

He'd send out an e-mail or two and make $5,000 or $10,000—sometimes even $20,000, or $40,000—from a little campaign. He was selling info products for under $100. He was selling a lot of them. He had a pretty decent-sized e-mail list.

The first time I saw him do this was right after he hired me. He sent an e-mail to his list talking about how he had hired me and how me selling him coaching got him inspired to create a program on how to sell services. Then he sold that program and basically made back how much he was spending on our coaching for the year. He made it back in an info product campaign from sending out a couple of e-mails to his list, all in a very short time.

I was excited that he had covered my fee already. It made me feel good that just from the intro session he had from me, he got so much value and he was able to then monetize that and make so much money back.

Over time, watching him do this over and over again, I started to get a little jealous. He was selling all this stuff and making all this money and I thought, "I should be able to do that. I feel like I have stuff to teach."

I remember I taught three teleclasses and recorded them, packaged them up and sold them online. It was actually my first info product I ever actually sold. It was $39. I sold only three copies.

I was devastated - instead of being excited about how I was starting to make money online from selling training programs.

A great thing about info products and training programs is you can create them, record them, and keep marketing them and making money from them for a long time without having to do a whole lot of extra work. You do some work with marketing, but a lot of that can be automated.

In retrospect, I wish I had been more excited when that happened. But I felt frustrated because I didn't make tens of thousands of dollars. My e-mail list at the time was probably only 400 people. I only sent one e-mail. What would have happened if I actually sent several e-mails or charged more? I was comparing myself to this other successful guy and I was really frustrated watching him make all the money.

I remember this moment clearly. I was standing on my balcony outside of my apartment in San Diego. I had been living here for only six or eight months at that point. I felt like I had so much stuff inside of me. I had been reading personal growth books since I was 13 years old and had all this training in NLP, hypnotherapy, and coaching.

I felt like I had so much to offer the world, but I didn't know how to get it out of me in a way that would get people to buy it—and buy lots of it. I was really frustrated because I felt like I had so much to offer and I wanted to get it out, and I felt like I was sitting on a million dollars.

Little did I know that I was actually sitting on multiple millions of dollars.

That's where my journey began -- to start learning online marketing and selling online. I was making around $40,000 a year in my coaching business, but I wasn't making anywhere near the kind of money I thought I could. Since I wasn't completely out of debt (I had about $35,000 in debt), making $40,000 a year in coaching while being able to do what I loved for a living was a huge accomplishment that I was very proud of and excited about. I loved being able to work for myself, but I felt like I wanted more.

I remember being out on my balcony feeling, "I can do this".

Then…

I don't know how to do this.

Who am I to do this?

I was having some doubts, but having this whole conversation in my mind. Even though I had some doubts, I still felt that if other people could do it, I could do it too.

I remember this line from a movie I like called "The Edge" with Anthony Hopkins and Alec Baldwin. They were being chased by bears and were talking about how younger men (or boys) would have to face a bear as a rite of passage and how they could kill the bear. Alec Baldwin said something like, "No, the bear is too big. It's too strong, too powerful. We can't kill the bear."

Then Anthony Hopkins said, "What one man can do, another man can do."

Well, what one woman can do, another woman can do. What one man can do, a woman can do. What a woman can do, a man can do—in most situations. (Obviously men can't have babies, but we certainly can help!)

So even though I had doubts, I decided to go for it. I didn't know where to turn first, but I made the commitment to do whatever it took to get all this stuff out of me into the world, to help lots of people and make lots of money.

The other thing I noticed at that time is that when I was working with a lot of clients, they'd have similar problems and challenges. I was already starting to think in terms of how I could help all of them.

Instead of having to teach the same thing to many different clients in many different coaching calls, if I had two or more clients struggling with the same thing, I would immediately create some sort of online solution for them. I would write an article about the topic or create a little audio teaching something about it. It wasn't a full-on hour-long class for sale, although every now and again I did that too.

I started seeing how a lot of people needed to learn more as well. So not only did they need the coaching, but they needed the training. I knew that people needed to learn this stuff and I just didn't know how to package it up. But I was committed to doing whatever it took to make it happen.

I started studying all kinds of marketing, and over the last many years, I've gone on to spend hundreds of thousands of dollars to learn about coaching, training, and specifically how to sell info products. A lot of marketing, a lot of business, and a lot of personal growth stuff is mixed into those hundreds of thousands of dollars as well.

One of the things I realized is not only do we need to know the "how to", but we also need the mindset and personal growth to become the kind of person who is able to become whatever it is you want to do—in this case, maybe a millionaire. To become a millionaire, you not only need the strategies, but you also need the mindset and you also need the personal growth to grow into a millionaire.

That's one of the reasons why people who win the lottery will oftentimes lose it all, because they didn't actually become a millionaire. They got a million dollars—or millions of dollars—but they didn't become a millionaire on the inside.

Since then, through the course of all my studies, I started launching programs. I remember the first big launch I did made $42,000 in 60 days. That was remarkable! The most money I ever made at a job was $35,000 in a year, and here I made $42,000 in 60 days. It was really exciting for me!

So I kept investing more money and I kept studying more and learning more. I kept doing more and more online launches and creating more online products. A few years after that, I hit a new benchmark and did $500,000 in sales in a launch. That was in 2009. I was obviously blown away by making $500,000 not only in a year, but to do $500,000 in sales in roughly one week.

Then just this past year, I did my biggest product launch ever and sold $1.1 million of one of my programs in eight days.

Over the years, I've made millions of dollars selling trainings. Mostly online training programs, but of course I've also made money selling tickets to live events. I've also made money selling coaching. There are lots of ways to help people. Coaching helps people in a really deep way, but information products, online training programs, video programs, and audio programs can help a wider group of people. That can add up to even more money and impact.

Over the years I've helped lots of people make money with info products. A very current example is one of my best friends who has also been a student of mine. He just had his best month ever, and made just under $25,000 in info product sales last month.

I love helping people become successful, and I want that for you too. As you keep reading this book I'm going to share all the best ideas that I've learned over the years through all of my experiences.

CHAPTER 5
Why People Buy and How to Make Things Sell

Why do people buy training programs? They want to learn something, right? Yes, that's true. But is it just that they want to learn something? No. They want to *change* something.

They want to change something—and they're in pain.

Usually it's all of those things, but at least some of those things need to be present. Obviously they want to learn something, but if they only want to learn something, how much money are they really going to invest? They might just go to the bookstore or library and look in a couple of books, or search online.

If they really want to change something, something different is happening. There's a difference between learning and changing. Learning is just about satisfying curiosity. Obviously learning can be applied to all kinds of things, but if people just want to learn something, they can look things up on the Internet.

If you want to really change something, however, you still might look stuff up on the Internet, but now it's about making things different. It's about achieving something, getting something, or getting out of pain.

I have invested tons of money over the years not only to help me grow my business, but also on my relationships. When I was single, I bought info products and went to seminars to learn about dating. Then I hired a coach to help me with dating. That helped me meet and marry the woman of my dreams. Now I have two kids. They act a little crazy sometimes. I recently invested just under $400 on a parenting training program, because I wanted to get my kids to behave better.

My kids are pretty young right now (3 ½ and 9 months), so it's not like there's anything crazy going on. No sex, drugs, and rock-n-roll or anything like that! For the most part, my kids are pretty well behaved, so I'm not in extreme pain. But I was in some pain and that was one of the things that led me to buying that program.

When it came to relationships, I felt the pain of being lonely for years. I dated a lot, but I was not in an exclusive, great relationship for four years straight and I was frustrated. So I bought a bunch of info products, attended seminars and even hired a coach to help me with that area of my life.

Pain is one of the biggest drivers. Pain is what drove me to want to learn all this stuff about info products. I saw other people being successful and I felt frustrated. I felt like I had all this stuff inside of me to share and I felt frustrated. I wanted to figure this stuff out and crack the code.

That's why people buy things.

If you want to sell something—if you want to sell a training program—then you need to sell something that helps people make changes, get out of pain, and achieve a goal of some sort.

Examples of this are helping people lose weight, helping people become thin and sexy, helping people find love, helping people start a business or grow a business, helping people turn a child's bad behavior around, helping people find a career that they love or helping them get hired or get promotions, helping people increase their sales, helping people become a better leader, better executive, better CEO, better manager, etc.

What kinds of things do people already want to change? Do you already have tools that can be used to help people make changes? If so, who could benefit from those changes? Who would really benefit the most? Who would benefit a lot by learning how to make those changes?

If you already have some tools, then you could start looking for a tribe. If you don't have the tools, you can also start looking for a tribe. A tribe is the group of folks who will buy your stuff like crazy. For me, for years, personal coaches and professional coaches have been my tribe.

It didn't start out that way. I started off just as a coach helping anyone with anything, and then eventually business owners and sales professionals started hiring me to help them. They were my top two biggest purchasers, so I niched myself as a business and sales coach. I eventually dropped the sales part. Although I still help people with sales, I focus on business owners.

Eventually, I started getting flooded with coaches wanting me to help them with their businesses, so eventually I decided to work specifically with personal coaches, professional coaches, business coaches, and coaches of all types.

Who is your tribe? Who would benefit most from your work? Is there a way to reach them as a group? Where do they hang out, in person or online? Do they already buy stuff in the subject area? Those are some big questions to ask, because if they do, then you have a good target market or tribe of folks who are already looking for leaders, already looking for changes, already looking for help. You'll want to reach out to these people.

Before we talk about how to reach out to these people and win them over, let's discuss how to pick a good tribe. Then I want to give you some ideas about how you can really make this work.

CHAPTER 6
These Folks Will Buy Your Stuff Like Crazy

If you have a skill, talent, or technique that could help anyone change anything—or if you don't have any skills, techniques, experience or ideas yet—you could still start off by just picking a group of people.

Either pick the group that could benefit most from your work, or pick a group that you're most interested in working with.

Maybe you have previous experience in that arena. Maybe you've been a sales professional and you could be a sales coach and teach some really great sales techniques. You could create an info product for sales professionals.

If you're a parent and you've learned a lot about parenting just by raising your own kids, you might have also read a bunch of books on parenting. You may already know things that could help a lot of parents.

Maybe you're really interested in relationships. You could help people with dating or you could help people who are already in relationships to help their relationship survive and thrive.

You could base it on the highest and best use. That's one way to pick your niche.

For example, think about the highest and best use in real estate. Let's say you have a house on the corner at a busy intersection. What's the most valuable use of that land? Is it to keep a house there? Is it to put up an apartment complex? Or what about a gas station, a grocery store or a convenience store? What would be the highest and best use of that land? Obviously when it comes to property, you have to fit in with the building codes and stuff like that, which sometimes restrict you from being able to build certain things there. What would you choose if you could choose anything?

At a busy intersection, maybe a gas station or convenience store might be the highest and best use. Let's say you own this property and you decide to sell your house. If you sell it to somebody who's just looking for a house, you might be able to sell it for whatever market value is. But if you sold it to somebody who could see the value of having a store there, then you might be able to sell it for twice as much, three times as much, five times as much, maybe ten times as much or possibly way more than that.

So if you had the same technique for helping someone overcome a fear, what fear could be the one that could make you the most money if you were able to help people overcome it? I can't answer this for you, but it's an interesting question.

Who would benefit the most from that? Who could pay the most for that? That's at least one factor to consider when picking your niche.

Obviously the other things to consider are your own past experience and your own interest level. It has to be something you're passionate about, because you're going to end up becoming one of the world's foremost experts on this topic. You're going to be spending a lot of time swimming and living in this subject matter, so make sure it's something that you are really interested in!

CHAPTER 7
Can YOU Really Make This Work?

The next thing that folks want to know is: can you really make this work?

What does it take to be successful selling training and coaching programs? Aside from the lack of marketing experience, I mentioned that I also had a lot of self-doubt. Things like…

Can I really do this?

Who am I to be a leader in this coaching industry?

Who am I to be a leader of any kind?

You may be having the same kind of thoughts. "Will people really buy stuff from me? Could I really make this happen? I'm not perfect yet."

First of all, I want to assure you that you don't have to be perfect.

None of us will ever be perfect unless you buy into the philosophy of perfect imperfection. With all of our imperfections, we're perfect just the way we are—that's my philosophy in life. The only way to ever be perfect is to be perfectly imperfect.

You don't have to be perfect and you don't have to have all the answers. You just need to be a little bit better than most folks out there, so you can help them along.

I've read that over 43% of people—and it could be even higher—never read a book after they finish college. 80% of US families did not buy even one book this year. These are staggering statistics. Most people don't read books, and don't continue educating themselves.

So if you read three books on any topic, you're already far ahead of the curve. You know way more about any given topic than 80-90% of the population out there. It sounds crazy, but it's true.

In the land of the blind, the one-eyed man is king. You don't have to be perfect. You don't have to have vision in both eyes. When you're leading people who don't have the answers, if you have just some of the answers, then people need you. You just need to be a little bit further along than most folks are so that you can teach them what you know.

You want to start not only thinking of yourself as an expert, but also as a leader. You want to take on a stewardship role over the group of people that you've now picked as your tribe. You want to become a leader of your tribe—a steward over your tribe. You want to take care of them. You want to nurture them. You might even make a mission out of helping people in your tribe.

If you are a weight loss expert, leader and coach, then your mission might be to help everyone on Earth who wants to be thin and stay thin, sexy and healthy to get thin, sexy and healthy and stay that way for the rest of their lives. That could be a really powerful guiding principle—a very powerful mission—for you. When you take on a mission like that, it changes a lot of the things that you do.

Now it's not just, "Hey, I want to sell some info products and make some money." It becomes, "I want to change the world. I want to help everyone who wants to be thin get thin, sexy and healthy and stay that way forever." That's powerful. That's going to shape and influence a lot of how you market your business, what you do in your business, what you stand for, what you say yes to and what you say no to.

People are hungry, and not just for information. They're hungry for leaders.

They are hungry for leaders that they can trust. There's so much information available out there on the Internet and in books, and it's hard to wade through all of that information to really figure out what to do.

So much of what's out there is people promising stuff that is not very realistic: the next pill to lose weight, the next fad diet to lose weight, or the newest crazy exercise. "If you just squeeze this thing between your thighs 20 times a day, all of a sudden you're going to lose 80 pounds miraculously! Watch how to do it!" Then in a little small font, they say "…and you have to be following our overall diet and exercise plan," because of course there's no way that pushing a thing between your legs is going to make a huge impact. But if it inspires people to exercise and have fun, if they do follow the exercise plan, then that's great too!

People are hungry for real information and real leaders they can trust. I want to be a role model of this for you by telling you that I've certainly done things that were much harder work than making money online. I've shoveled concrete. I've delivered mattresses by myself. I remember delivering this king-sized mattress all by myself one day and had to go up flights of stairs. I've had jobs that were a lot more challenging than my online training business—but that doesn't mean that they were harder overall.

Some of these jobs were more challenging physically, but when you have your own business, it challenges you mentally; it challenges you emotionally. It forces you to grow. You have to be a self-starter. You're not going to necessarily have a boss, but you'll probably have a coach. Of course the coach isn't the same as a boss, but at least they can help you stay on track— which I highly recommend. I think everybody should have a coach. If you want to achieve anything spectacular in this world, I would highly recommend having a coach to do it.

Even with a coach, you are your own boss and that presents its own challenges. You don't have somebody breathing down your neck, which is great. But it also can be tough because you do have to be a self-starter. You have to be an action taker.

What happens when you send your first e-mail out and no one buys your program? That can be devastating. For me, I had only three people buy my very first program, and instead of being excited about it, I was devastated by it.

I had just finished a $1.1 million launch in December and I had two back to back two-day live events in January, and on the fourth day of my second live event, I burst into tears on stage.

Unfortunately they were not tears of joy. I just had done my biggest launch ever. I had just launched my first bestselling book, and here I was on stage crying. I was crying because I felt that, in spite of everything, I still didn't feel good enough.

Unconsciously, I had been feeling that if I just made enough money, if I just got enough people to my seminars, if I was friends with the right kinds of people—the super-successful people—then I'd be good enough.

And here I was. I had just done a $1.1 million launch and had a bestselling book and I still didn't feel like I was good enough. I burst out in tears on stage. I actually went on a long rant and told everyone in the audience what I was feeling. "If I was just this, I'd be good enough." "If I wore just the right clothes, I'd be good enough." "If I just made people laugh enough, I'd be good enough." "If I just gave away enough great valuable stuff for free, then I'd be good enough."

Money isn't the solution to all of life's problems, although we often think it is. Money is a great thing to have in our lives. But whenever you're going for something big and you're doing something big, it's going to challenge you in ways that you might not expect.

I remember when my income first jumped from around $100,000 a year to around $250,000 a year. It was from one month to the next. I went from making around $8,500 a month to making around $25,000 a month. It felt really weird and made me feel really uncomfortable.

I know that sounds crazy. I'm giving you all these examples of success making me feel uncomfortable, but I'll tell you that of course failures have made me uncomfortable too.

I remember my $42,000 launch. When I made $42,000 in 60 days, I felt like I should have made $1 million—and I only made $42,000. I don't know where I got this crazy expectation.

I know, I'm obviously pretty mentally disturbed to have all of these challenges, but in my experience coaching business owners for the last 13 or 14 years, we're all crazy! All of us. That's okay. That's just part of the human condition. It's part of our perfect imperfection.

I share all this with you for two reasons. Number one, to admit my flaws and that I'm still a work in progress and that I'm not perfect, and in spite of that, I'm still going out there and creating info products and helping people. People are getting great results and I'm helping to change a lot of lives.

I'm also sharing this with you so that you know it isn't always easy. It can be a huge test. You're going to have to learn some technology stuff or hire some people that can help you with technology. You're going to have to become not only the leader of your tribe but also the leader of your business, and you have to begin bringing other people on board. For me, that's been one of the most fun things about my business—having a team of people who help me. They get to do the stuff they love and I get to do the stuff I love.

In the early days, I remember one time I was lying in bed for a whole week straight just feeling miserable, and letting myself feel miserable. It was the impetus for one of my powerful personal growth techniques that I teach people called "The Peace Process", which you'll find at the end of this book.

It was an early edition to that process. Instead of taking minutes, back then it took me about a week. It was a really big, heavy bunch of stuff I had piled on myself. I felt like I should just be able to make all the success happen by myself. I shouldn't need a team. I was just being lazy because I wasn't able to launch products and make all this big money all by myself. I felt like I needed people's help. I was ashamed of that. I was judging myself and felt it was wrong for me to not be able to just do it all by myself.

Finally, after about a week of that, I got to the other side and felt that it was totally okay. One of my clients I had mentioned earlier who was really successful with his own products, he did everything by himself. I'm happy to report that, years later, my business is probably at least three or four times bigger than his businesses and it's because I overcame those challenges and built a team. He's still doing everything by himself. That's his Achilles Heel. He can't give up control—or he hasn't been able to yet. I don't know how seriously he's worked on himself on that. I think, on some level, he really enjoys doing a lot of it by himself.

My Achilles Heel of feeling like I needed to do it all by myself and being ashamed and frustrated that I couldn't actually has become one of my greatest strengths now that I've made peace with the fact that I have not created everything—and that's okay.

You don't have to be great at everything either. You could be great at research. My wife is a really great researcher. She loves researching. If you're good at researching, you can figure out a lot of these different pieces of the puzzle to put together to make a great program. You may already have great ideas anyway, and that's good too.

One of my super strengths is being able to teach. I could almost teach anything, even if it was something I didn't even know anything about. Somehow I'm just able to channel or intuit great ideas to share with other people.

Other people are just really good at coaching people and have processes for that, and if you could teach those processes and apply them to a specific topic you could be really successful. Some people are really strong at the marketing side, but aren't necessarily strong teachers. They can develop that side or partner with somebody.

There are always ways to be successful. The key to success is to decide on what you want and then never give up on making it happen. That's the key to success. Whatever it is that you want, make it a must—not a want to, not a like to, not a should do - but an absolute must. When you make something a must, things change. You start finding the resources. Things start to shift inside of you.

When I first started to coach, I just wanted to be able to match the kind of money I made at my job and be able to do that as a coach. Within two or three years, I was able to do that. But of course that income wasn't enough, because then I got myself $72,000 in debt—so now I actually needed more money than that.

Then I sold my house and moved to California. I lowered my expenses. I had money in the bank. I still had some debt, but I was happy living that way for a while making that kind of money until all of a sudden I wasn't happy anymore. I got really frustrated. I wanted to make more money. I wanted to make six figures.

Then I made six figures and decided I wanted to make $250,000. At some point I decided I wanted to make a million. I wanted to be a millionaire, and I made that a must. Eventually I got there. Money isn't everything, of course, but it certainly helps us have a great life. Becoming a millionaire challenged me in so many ways, and it forced me to deal with a bunch of things about myself.

Having a great relationship was a must for me. I studied lots of training programs for that and hired coaches for that and met my wife eight years ago.

Whatever you want, make it a must and keep going after it until you get it. That's a great way to be a leader in your own life, in addition to being a leader for your tribe.

CHAPTER 8
How To Build An E-mail List Of Hot Prospects

The next thing I want to share with you is how to build an e-mail list of hot prospects. Once you know what your tribe is, now you need to build up a database (an e-mail list) of your tribe. There are several ways to do that.

The first thing you want to is potentially create an info product that you can give away for free. This could be an article, a video or an audio. It could be a software or tool. It doesn't necessarily matter what format it's in. It just needs to be something of extreme value to your tribe.

One of the things I give away to my list is a script or swipe e-mail copy people can e-mail to their list if they have one—or if not, to their friends and family or post it on a blog page and tweet or Facebook about it. It's copy that they can use to attract coaching clients. They can just send it out to their e-mail list and get a bunch of people wanting to work with them, to "make the phone ring."

In our modern Internet age, it's really to make the inbox zing and say, "You've got mail," from somebody who really wants to work with you—not just your regular e-mail.

That script is really valuable. It gets people results that they hadn't been getting before. In my tribe, a lot of coaches will do all kinds of marketing stuff—they'll even start growing a bit of an e-mail list, but they don't really make any specific offer to people to work with them. By using my script, all of a sudden they get a rush of interest. That's one of the things I give away instantly when people get on my e-mail list. Of course there are other articles, videos, and tools that I've created over the years that I give my list for free as well.

I want you to start thinking about what you could teach your list that would be the most powerful thing that you could teach them and that would be mind-blowingly valuable. Something that would make you feel a bit scared to give it away for free - something that valuable.

I had a coach when I was first really getting rocking with my info product type stuff. I remember I was writing a lot of articles and my coach at the time was telling me, "Whoa, you're going too far and giving away too much. You're giving away the whole story here in your e-mails."

I felt like if I'm making him nervous, then that might be a good sign. I wanted to create the most valuable e-mail newsletter for coaches on Earth—if not the most valuable newsletter, period. So I started writing articles sharing all of my best ideas that I possibly could in those e-mails and I started sending them out.

My list was under 500 people. I started sending those out, and just from word of mouth, people started sending it to other people and my list started growing. Also, I declared that I was going to be the leader of the coaching industry, even before I created info products, even before I was making six figures, and within a few months I got a phone call from a writer at *Forbes Magazine* wanting to interview me about coaching.

I was in this place where I was having a down day about business, life or who knows what and I got this call. It went to my voicemail. I listened to my voicemail and thought, "Oh, wow, this is a great opportunity." But I thought, "Man, I'm just not in a good place right now. I'll call tomorrow when I'm feeling a little bit better." That was my first instinct.

Then my second thought was, "This guy isn't going to wait until tomorrow. He wants to get his questions answered today. I have to call him right now no matter how I feel."

He left this message wanting to know specific information. I rustled up some info and called him back, and this way I could give him all the stuff that I had. I asked him to put my website in the article as a hyperlink because it was going to be an online article. I asked, "Can you put a hyperlink to my website in the article?"

He said, "No, I can't do that."

I asked, "Could you at least put my website name, even if it's not a hyperlink?"

He said, "I don't know if I can do that. If I can, I will. But I can't promise anything."

When I asked him to do that, my website wasn't even up yet. But by declaring to the universe that you're willing to become a leader or that you're on a mission of some sort, the universe conspires in your favor.

This guy ended up posting the article and put my website URL into the article. It wasn't hyperlinked, but I ended up getting some good subscribers from that. Then it got picked up by Yahoo! Then it got picked up by MSN, and on MSN, anything with a dot-com at the end automatically gets hyperlinked. So that obviously helped me grow my e-mail list a little bit.

Declaring that you're going to become the leader or a steward for a group of people is powerful. Declaring anything that you want to the universe is powerful. The universe wants to give you whatever it is that you want. Now, you may have to grow a lot to get it, and your path to success may be a winding one, but anything is possible. Whatever you want wants you.

Back to how to grow your list. You want to think about something you can give away for free. Maybe it's a free teleclass or a free special report. What's one thing you could give away right now—one idea, one strategy, one technique?

For me, the thing that I mentioned that I give away is swipe copy. People could just copy/paste and send it to their list. That's a tool. It's something they can just have. I teach people to make a really compelling free coaching session offer. But instead of just teaching people how to do that, I thought, "Let me go another step further, because a lot of times when I teach people how to do this, then they write ones that aren't so hot. They try to do it, but they don't do it as well as I could do it. Why don't I just write one for every major niche market for coaches and then just give that away?" It's done for you. I did the work for that so I could give something away that is incredibly valuable.

Think outside the box. What could you do to give something away that would be valuable? Then, if you're giving something away that's valuable, how can you take it to the next level to make it even more valuable?

A lot of people don't want to give away their best secrets for free, thinking, "If I give away the best stuff for free, what would they pay me for?"

Maybe my best idea was to give away these free session offers, but then actually having them done for you is even better. Even in doing that, that doesn't necessarily solve every coach's problem. Now they need to learn how to sign up clients for an intro session. That's my number one best-selling product: "Free Sessions That Sell." (www.FreeSessionsThatSell.com)

But they also need to learn marketing. I have another program for that called "Client Attraction and Money Making Mastery." (www.ClientAttractionAndMoneyMakingMastery.com)

They may also need to learn how to do the coaching. Maybe they want to get better at coaching. I have a program for that called "Rapid Coaching Academy." (www.RapidCoachingAcademy.com)

Maybe they want to learn how to form joint venture partnerships to get other people to promote them. I have a program for that called "High Profit JV Partnerships". (www.HighProfitJVPartnerships.com)

They'll want to learn how to create a business plan for their coaching business. I have a program for that called "Coach's Business Plan Tool Kit". (http://coachingsuccessuniversity.com/programs/bizplan/)

If they want to learn how to create marketing materials, I have a program for that called "Coach's Marketing Materials Master Class." (http://coachingsuccessuniversity.com/programs/copy/)

Maybe they want to learn how to do group coaching. I have a program for that called "Group Coaching Goldmine." (http://coachingsuccessuniversity.com/programs/gcg/)

Perhaps they want to learn how to create info products. I have a training for that called "Make Your Programs Make You Millions." (www.MakeYourProgramsMakeYouMillions.com)

If they want to learn how to grow their list, I have a program for that called "Big List." (http://coachingsuccessuniversity.com/programs/get-big-list/)

And on and on and on.

So as you can see from my example, giving away your best thing for free does not in any way give them everything they could possibly ever want to learn about your topic. You can give them your best weight loss secret for free. You can give them your best dating secrets for free.

What's "the best" thing to give away? You want to think in terms of not only what would help them the most, but also what they think would help them the most. Oftentimes those can be two very different things.

For example, I might think what they need the most is to learn how to sell coaching. That's probably true. But what they may think they need to learn the most is where to find clients.

Or if somebody wants to have success with dating, you might think what they most need to learn is how to have more confidence in themselves and confidence with women. But what they think they might need is a pick-up line. "If I just had the right pick-up line, I could get a girl's phone number."

You want to give people not just the thing that would help them the most, but the thing they think would help them the most. Keep that in mind.

With everything that we do, we want to keep our target market in mind.

What are they thinking? What do they want? How are they being challenged? What are their biggest pains, problems, challenges, dreams, desires, irrational fears and fantasies? What's really going on inside their minds? The more you know about what's going on inside their minds, the better you can help them and the better you can market to them.

Growing an e-mail list of hot prospects is going to happen once you've identified your tribe and you know where they hang out and you know where you can reach them. Then you have something really valuable to give them. Then you can start telling people, "You can get this thing for free by entering your name and e-mail address here." You can tell people about it on Facebook. You could advertise and tell people about it. You could form strategic alliances or joint venture partnerships. JVs are a great way to grow your list.

Some people love advertising as a great way to grow your list—getting pay-per-click ads or Facebook ads or other types of advertising to grow their e-mail list. That's great! I personally like doing joint ventures. It's one of my strengths. I like partnering with people.

Find other people who already have an e-mail list of the people you want to reach, and then you can talk to them about how you can work together. I have a whole program on this called "High Profit JV Partnerships" (www.HighProfitJVPartnerships.com) that teaches you how to identify who would make a great strategic alliance partner for you (or JV partner), how to get yourself JV ready and if you approach a JV partner and they said yes, you would have all your systems in place. It shows you how to reach out to JV partners and how to get that conversation started. Then it teaches you how to win them over to agree to promote you. Then it teaches you how to have a successful co-promotion so they think it was really valuable that they promoted you and they want to do it again.

Those are all the things that you'll want to do. You'll want to know how to reach out to people. I'll share a couple of ideas with you right out of the gate. One of the best ways to reach people to win them over is to ask them how you can best help them. Instead of reaching out to them saying, "Hey, will you promote my stuff?" if you want them to promote your stuff, one of the best ways of doing that is to reach out to them and say, "How can I best help you? How can I help you get more customers? How can I help you get more clients?"

Or even something completely unrelated to that. Sometimes I've coached someone who would be a great strategic alliance partner for me. I just coach them for free as a way to help build rapport and build a relationship. Then at some point, they ask, "Wow. How can I help you?"

Of course, depending on where you are in your business, you don't want to just be coaching everybody for free and then hoping that one day they're going to ask you to promote you. It doesn't have to be like that.

That's just one way, especially when you're getting started, if you have the ability to coach people—if you have some ways that you can help other people—then that's a really smart way to build that relationship.

CHAPTER 9
How to Create Training Programs

Before you create your training program, one thing you might want to do is survey your list to find out what it is they most want to learn about a certain topic. What are their biggest challenges about a topic? What's the name they most like? For example, for this book, I surveyed my list to find out the book title they resonated with the most.

Once you know what they're looking for, name your program something really hot and compelling—something very powerful that makes them want to buy the program just because of the name.

My info product "Make Your Programs Make You Millions," is already, just by the name alone, very compelling.

One of my programs was named "Coaching Business Rocket Launcher Live" and that wasn't so hot. Then I thought, "What does this teach people? It teaches people marketing. I'll name it Coach's Marketing Mastery Program."

Then I realized that people don't really want to learn marketing. They just want to get clients and make money. So instead of it being "Coaching Business Rocket Launcher" or "Coaching Business Marketing Mastery" I decided to call it "Client Attraction and Money Making Mastery." It's really about getting clients and getting money and not about the marketing. Marketing is really just a necessary step to get the results.

You want to name your program something compelling.

There are two different kinds of programs you can create. You can create a master class mastery program like "Client Attraction and Money Making Mastery". It teaches you everything you need to know about that. Or you could teach something that's more of a specific topic, like my "Free Sessions That Sell" program, that teaches people specifically how to do introductory coaching sessions.

If you're a weight loss coach, you could create a program on how to lose weight, or you could sell a product specifically on one element, like how to eliminate food cravings. Either way, it's totally okay. There are some pros and cons to both, but either one is totally cool.

Once you know what the scope of your program is going to be—whether it's going to be a bigger program or a more self-contained micro-topic—then you can start creating your program.

If you were creating a whole program on weight loss, you'd need to identify the biggest challenges with losing weight. You'd create your program around the steps people would need to follow to overcome those challenges and lose the weight they want.

I need to know what kind of exercise I should be doing. I need to know what kind of food I should be eating (or shouldn't be eating). I need to know how to eliminate food cravings and handle emotional eating, stress eating, and binge eating. I need to know how to get extra support and join a community of other people who want to lose weight.

Whatever these things are for your topic, you need to figure it out and outline the major steps. If it's a more micro program like how to eliminate food cravings, maybe a 5 or 7 step process. I would just outline those seven steps and teach that 7-step process.

For something as small scoped as eliminating food cravings, that might just be a one-shot teleclass. If it's bigger and more comprehensive like "Free Sessions That Sell," it isn't just one class. It's a 5-session program, but it's way smaller and shorter than "Client Attraction and Money Making Mastery," which is a much more comprehensive program. Then each of the modules is broken down into those five or seven steps.

You need a beginning. Anytime you're going to teach something, you want to give an introduction. In this book, I talked about my journey, how I got started with info products, how I've been successful with info products, how I've helped other people with info products and how I'm going to share my best ideas with you.

If you were going to do an introduction for weight loss, you might tell your story about how you used to be overweight if you were, how you've lost that weight and kept it off forever and now how you help other people to do that.

You want to have an introduction that explains who you are and why you're teaching this stuff. If you're selling something, now that people have your program, you want to re-sell them and tell them all the benefits they're going to get. If they're going to lose weight and be healthy, thin, and sexy forever, then talk about what it feels like to be healthy, thin, and sexy forever. It might mean people of the opposite sex starting to look at you and smile at you more often. It means you get this attention and that attention.

Sometimes that can be unwanted attention, which is one of the reasons why people tend to gain weight in the first place. They're trying to not get that attention because it makes them feel uncomfortable. So you could tell them, "That's one of the things we'll work on the program: how to get comfortable being thin, healthy, and sexy forever. But the other benefits are this, this, this, and that.

The challenges with being overweight are ridiculous. It's so frustrating to have to do this, and if you look in the mirror and you don't want to have sex with the lights on and you don't want this or that, I'm going to teach you all this stuff and help you turn your life around starting right now.

Here's the overview of the program. We're going to cover these five things: this, this, this, this, and that. Let's get started!"

Then, boom! You move right into the first module, second module, third module, fourth module, and fifth module to teach your content. After you teach everything, you wrap everything up with a conclusion recapping everything that you've taught.

Certainly if it's a live program, you can have Q&A along the way. But you don't have to include Q&A at all.

You could wrap things up by wishing them well. "I wish you well on your journey. I hope you go for it, lose all the weight, and keep it off forever."

In this case as we are discussing creating your own info products, I would say that I really hope you decide to go for it and create your info products and help a lot of people. There are people all over the world who are struggling and suffering right now because they don't know the answers to the problems that they have and they don't know who to listen to. They're looking for a leader. They're looking for you, and you can help them. I really hope you do.

All over the world right now people are struggling and suffering because they don't have your help and they don't have your leadership, and they maybe don't even know it yet. You could be helping those people and prospering in your own life like never before. I really hope you decide to go for it. If you do decide to go on this journey, then I'd love to help you take things to the next level.

I hope you consider looking into some of my additional support programs like the "Make Your Programs Make You Millions" training (www.MakeYourProgramsMakeYouMillions.com), the "Big List" training (http://coachingsuccessuniversity.com/programs/get-big-list/), the "High Profit JV Partnerships" training (www.HighProfitJVPartnerships.com) or potentially working with me personally to help you achieve these kinds of results and create your own info product empire, or working with one of the coaches on my team.

If you decide to help lots of people and make lots of money, I wish you the best on your journey and I hope you will keep me posted on your success. Until we meet in person—or until we meet again—keep helping people, keep serving people, and keep smiling. God bless.

There's how you could wrap something up. That was my example of a wrap up.

CHAPTER 10
How To Sell Your Info Product

If you want to have a successful information product business, then you've got to have a lot of pieces in place.

You have to have the confidence in yourself and the trust in yourself to be a leader of a tribe. You have to reach out to them with something of extreme value and you have to win them over and get them on your e-mail list. You can do that in a variety of ways. Certainly advertising, joint ventures, public speaking, and networking are great ways to build your e-mail list. These are all things that I teach super in-depth inside my training program called "Big List." For me, joint ventures have been one of the hottest ways to grow my list and sell a lot of my trainings.

You also need to have a system for selling things. You need to have a sales system. There are basically three ways to sell things, and there are a lot of campaigns that you can create.

Here's how to sell your info product:

1. **Through one-on-one conversations**

You can sell info products through one-on-one sales conversations—what I call free sessions that sell. It's a great way to sell high-end coaching, but if you also have training programs, if they don't buy your one-on-one coaching, then you could offer them just the training program and still make a sale where you otherwise might not have been able to.

For example, if you're selling coaching for, say, $1000 a month for six months, and people say, "I can't afford that," or "I'd love to work with you, but there's no way I can swing that right now," then you can say, "I have another program that might be a better fit for your budget. Would you like to hear a little bit about that?" If they say yes, then you could tell them about your training program and potentially sell that to them.

So that's one way to sell things—through one-on-one conversations. That's great if you're already going to be doing those sessions to sell high-end coaching. If you're already going to be selling your high-end packages, then it's great because if people don't buy your one-on-one coaching, now you have something else to sell them.

One-on-one is always the highest conversion. You might sell between 40% of the people to as much as 80% of the people—even 100%, depending on how you pre-quality folks. That's going to be the highest converting way to sell anything.

2. Through public speaking

The second highest way to sell anything is through public speaking. You teach something either in person or on a teleclass or webinar. You teach some great content, and then you sell some of your trainings. That's the second-highest converting way to sell things.

From that style of selling, you could expect maybe between 5% on the low end to as much as 40%, depending on the price of your offer and how qualified the folks are on your teleclass. You may even get up to 80% of the people to buy if it's not priced super high.

Selling from a teleclass, webinar or in-person training, generally people will sell in the 20-30% range. It's anywhere between 5-60% is on average, but 20-30% is probably more in line with what most people are doing these days, although it can vary.

3. Through a sales letter or video

The least effective way to sell is to just have a sales letter or sales video where people watch a video and you sell something or they read a letter and you sell something. Typically sales letters and sales videos convert between half-a-percent on the really low end to as much as 12% on the really, really high end. On average, between 2-8% of the people who go to a page will buy from a sales letter or video.

So here's the question…why would anybody do anything except one-on-one conversations? If selling one-on-one is the highest converting, why would people choose to do it some other way?

It's because it takes somebody on the phone actually having to reach out and talk to prospects. Your time is limited. Your prospect's time is limited. It's the highest converting, but least efficient. It takes time to do these sessions.

If you're selling coaching, this is great, because just from a couple of clients, you can actually make a huge amount of money. It's worth doing. Certainly we still do it in our business.

Selling from teleclasses, webinars and live events is more efficient. Your conversion rate is probably going to go down a bit, but you can do one talk and get 30, 40, 50 or even hundreds of people—even thousands of people—at a time. So even though you're converting at a lower rate, those numbers really add up.

In one hour with one prospect, you might make one sale, which is awesome. Even if your conversion rate was always 100%, you'd have only one sale from one hour of talk. Even if it was one sale in a half hour, that would be great. If you're converting at 100%, if you do two one-on-one sessions back to back, in one hour, you make two sales.

But if you had 1,000 people on a teleclass, and if you were able to convert 5% of those people who are on the call live with you (which would be a little bit on the low end), that's 50 sales.

I have done teleclasses with thousands of people on the line. It's taken me years to get my business to this point, so I wouldn't expect everybody to have thousands of people on the line in the beginning. But you can certainly get dozens of people, or maybe even hundreds of people, or maybe 1,000 people on a call. Selling that way is great.

A lot of people will register for a call, but how many people will actually show up for a call? Usually the number is about 20-25% of the people who register that actually show up. There are ways to increase that. You can get that to 40-60%.

Also, it's the law of diminishing numbers. The bigger the number is, usually the lower the conversions are. If you have a small list, 40 or 60% of the people on your list could actually show up for your teleclass. As your list gets to be thousands of people and tens of thousands—maybe even hundreds of thousands of people—then the percentages usually tend to go down. It's not always true, but it's a generalization to be aware of. But it doesn't matter, because as you get bigger and bigger numbers, then you also get bigger and bigger numbers of sales.

If you're selling something from a sales letter or sales video, now your numbers go down even more in terms of percentages, but more people have the opportunity to see your message. If you send out an e-mail to your list with a sales letter or sales video on it, instead of clicking to register for a teleclass, waiting for the day of the teleclass and showing up on the line for that teleclass and then potentially buying or not buying, now people can click and immediately start watching your video or reading your sales letter. You're going to get a higher volume of people watching or reading those things.

Even though now the conversion rates go down, you're reaching more people. It's more leveraged, too, because you don't have to do a teleclass and another teleclass and another teleclass. You can just create your video once or write your sales letter once, and then lots of people can see it.

Those are the three ways to sell something. The sales process is a little different with each one.

But it all comes down to one powerful formula, and I'm going to share that formula with you right now. That formula involves talking about what people most want on your topic.

Let's say you're a dating, weight loss coach, business coach, etc. and you have an offer for some big result.

"Now You Can Really Lose All The Weight You Want And Keep It Off Forever Following This Simple 3-Step System" might be a headline. Then you tell them what the simple 3-step system is.

In a one-on-one selling conversation, you want people to tell you what their goals are, but when you're selling to a group, then you should already know what their goals are and present an offer that helps them achieve their goals *and* that helps them overcome their challenges.

For example, if I were selling a product on how to create info products, I'd be talking about some of the stuff I've already mentioned in this book. I'd start talking about dreams of info products and how info products can make you lots of money and this can change your lifestyle. You could live like I do and work about 20 hours a week and have a team of people who do all the work that you don't love and you can just show up and do the fun stuff. Info products can give you the money to buy fancy cars and live in a nice house in exactly the place that you would want to live. I live in San Diego, California, which is one of the greatest places on Earth. You can take lots of vacations. You can save money for retirement or your kids' education. You can buy your parents a house if you want to—whatever you want to do.

Talk about the dream of what's possible for your particular topic. Then you talk about the challenges.

At the beginning of this book, I talked about how I was frustrated. I was $35,000 in debt. I had to have a roommate to live out here in San Diego because the cost of living was higher than when I lived in Chicago. I was driving a car that was kind of old and starting to break down. I had grown up poor when I was a kid and felt the bonds of that, and I had friends who were making more money than I was and I felt frustrated about it. I had all this stuff inside me I knew I wanted to share and I didn't know how to get it out to teach other people—but I knew I wanted to.

Then I tried to do it on my own and failed. I couldn't make much money. I did my first launch and it made me almost nothing. I was frustrated because I didn't know how to do all this stuff myself and I felt like I really needed to.

I had all this pent-up energy. I didn't know how to do it, but I just knew that I wanted to—and I knew I would find a way. And I decided I would find a way and do whatever it would take and invest whatever I needed to invest.

Over the course of several years, I've invested hundreds of thousands of dollars to learn how to do all the stuff that has given me the lifestyle that I live now—and most of that is related to selling online training programs.

I'd like to help you learn how to sell online training programs, too, if you're interested in living this kind of a lifestyle. I'm going to be honest with you, I can't guarantee everybody is going to get there. I will tell you that most people won't, because most people won't do what it takes. Most people won't study my trainings. Most people won't implement. Most people won't make it a must.

But I'll tell you, if you make it a must, you will get there—if you're willing to do the work, if you're willing to grow personally. I don't know how long it will take. For some people, it might take years. It's taken me a long time to get to the place where I'm making millions of dollars. But some people do it a lot faster. Some people might be able to do it within a year. That's not a promise by any stretch, but I know some people would be able to do it.

But however much money you make, it will be worth it. It will be worth it not only for the money, but it will also be worth it for the growth and the kind of person you become along the way. Then after you describe their goals and challenges you'll say, "If you're interested in joining me, then I'd love to tell you the details of my program."

Then you tell them about your program.

"This program is five modules. We cover this, this, this, and that. This is what it would do for you. This is how it's going to help you. And this is the investment. I've invested hundreds of thousands of dollars over the years, but your investment will be $X. You don't have to pay $200,000. You don't have to pay $50,000 like you would for a college education that probably wouldn't make you as much money as this will. You would just have to pay $X." You can do some comparison pricing.

Then you need the call-to-action.

"Here's what to do next. Go to dadadada.com and decide whether you want to do the full-pay option or whether you want to do the payment plan. Go order now." Or "Click the button below and order now."

That's how to sell your programs. That's the sales formula. I outlined it above, and now I'll just break it down for you.

1. Talk about what it is people most want first (or let them talk about it if it's an intro session).

2. Talk about the challenges and frustrations people are going through by either not having it or trying to do it on their own and not getting the results they want.

3. Talk about your solution and how your solution can help them get what they want and overcome their challenges.

4. Give them the details of the program and how each aspect of the program is going to help them achieve a component of the result that they're looking for and help them overcome some of the related challenges.

For example, if you were teaching weight loss, you might just have a simple 3-step system. Step 2 in your system might be eliminating food cravings, and you might have a little section talking about how food cravings often destroy diets more than anything else. "What happens when you're on a diet and you're doing well for a little while?"

"Maybe you've done well for three days or maybe you've done well for ten days, but then all of a sudden somebody shows you a food and you end up running across the food either in your house or out and public somewhere that you almost can't say no to. I know for me it's dark chocolate. I love it. The only thing worse than dark chocolate is free dark chocolate. Free dessert is always more compelling. It's easier to say no to dessert when you also have to pay for it, but when it's free right in front of you, it's hard to say no."

"But I discovered a secret years ago that helped me eliminate food cravings and actually become strong enough to say no to dark chocolate, and I'm going to share that with you inside Module 2, which is Overcoming Food Cravings."

See how you would break that down into each module talk about each piece of it?

5. Tell them what the investment is.

Before you give them the investment, you want to have a comparison price. Your comparison price can be how much it would cost with you one-on-one. "My clients pay me $100,000 a year or more to work with me personally. But you're not going to have to invest $100,000 a year."

Your comparison price might be what you've invested to learn all this stuff or your comparison price could be how much people generally spend to try to lose weight before they actually ever do it—if they ever do. "Most people will spend this much money to lose weight. They do plastic surgery, liposuction, and all these things to try to lose weight which all add up to this amount of money. And what happens to a lot of people who get liposuction? If they haven't changed their diet, oftentimes they go right back to the same weight. Then of course there's the cost of food and medical expenses for being unhealthy."

You have all these comparison costs. Talk about how not only does your program not cost what all those things cost, but it's going to save you money from what you would have otherwise spent to try to achieve your goal, only to most likely never actually get the results that you want.

"So instead, you can invest $1997 and learn how to lose weight, and be thin, healthy, and sexy forever."

Is that worth $2,000? Yes, it is. Especially when you can compare it to really expensive things. Now, will everybody pay $2,000? No. But that's okay. The people who do invest that amount are going to be a lot more committed and much more likely to get results.

I'm not saying exactly how anybody should price their programs. That's something for you to decide. I'd recommend you test different prices. If you sell something at $2,000, you might make more money per copy, but you might sell a little bit less. However, if you sell it for $500 per copy, are you going to sell four times as many or do you only sell twice as many? If you sell twice as many copies at $500 as you do at $2000, you should probably sell it at $2,000.

If you sell 10 copies at $500, that would be $5,000. If you sell 100 copies at $500, that would be $50,000. But if you sold half as many (50 at $2,000), then that would be $100,000. You'd make twice as much money even though you only sell half as much. Price your program for maximum profit.

If you have a guarantee, you also want to tell people what your guarantee is. Is it 30 days, 15 days? Is there no guarantee at all?

That's the formula for selling programs.

There are also additional ways to make things sell. Events sell things. If you want to sell a lot more stuff, you could sell things by having a product launch—an event that will help you sell a lot more of a product. Having a 50% off sale or something like that helps to sell more stuff. Having a "price going up" event sells more stuff. "These are the last three days to get this program before the price doubles" or "before there's a significant increase." That's an event that drives sales. Including special bonuses could be an event that drives sales.

I created "Free Sessions That Sell" as an info product. That was my first very successful—and still my most successful—info product. In the early days, I decided to offer a live Q&A call. I said, "If you want to get my program and be on the live Q&A call, order this program."

That was before I did any of these other things. I didn't do product launches. I didn't do sales. I didn't do prices going up events. That was my first event to drive more sales—and it worked. It's not necessarily as hot as some of these other strategies, but it's powerful.

Events drive sales. Once you create a product, think about what kind of event you're willing to do to help drive more sales. This is true in regular stores, too. Think about all the sales stores are having all the time: a Memorial Day sale, a President's Day sale, a Black Friday sale. All those things drive sales.

What percentage of revenue is made on those sale days? We all know Black Friday, the day after Thanksgiving, is called Black Friday because that's the day that most people get out of the red and into the black. Maybe they're losing money all year, and then finally on that day, that's when they make most of their money and they get out of the red and into the black.

That's a momentous day of selling for salespeople. If you had a program that sits available all the time for sale like I do, you'll make sales every now and again depending on your price. Events can help you drive sales even more at higher price points, too. That's something important to keep in mind.

When one of my programs was $1,000, people would buy it on their own through my e-mail marketing campaigns or friends would tell them about it and they'd read the sales letter and buy it. When we raised the price to $1,997, that wasn't happening anymore. People weren't just randomly buying it on their own. When we did events, people would still buy it at $1,997 and we would make twice as much money.

Keep in mind events will not only drive sales, but they'll help you be able to charge even more for your product than you might have otherwise been able to. Events are a powerful way to drive sales.

CHAPTER 11
Putting It All Together

Now you know the formula to help lots of people and make lots of money with your training. Let's do a quick review.

You're going to want to remember why people buy things and how to make things sell. People want to change something. They're in pain. They want to get out of that pain. They want to achieve something. Then if you want to sell something, you need to create programs that are specific for certain people to achieve certain results that they're already looking for.

You want to build up a tribe of folks who will buy yourself like crazy—people who would benefit from your work, people who you can reach as a group. They hang out together either in person or online. They're already willing to buy stuff in that subject area.

Choose a topic that you're passionate about and then step up and be a leader of your tribe. You don't have to be perfect to make this happen. You don't have to have all the answers. In the land of the blind, the one-eyed woman is queen. People are looking for information, but they're also looking for leaders that they can trust. And you can be that leader.

You want to build a list of hot prospects by advertising, public speaking, networking, hanging out in person or online where your target market hangs out or through joint ventures. You're going to give away something really valuable for free to get people onto your e-mail list.

Once people are on your e-mail list, then you can continue nurturing that relationship with them and make special offers to them—things that are going to be extremely valuable to them, things that they're already looking for.

Finding JV partners is one of the hot ways to grow your list. You can reach out to them. You want to identify who else sells to your target market. How can you reach them? Are you ready to be promoted by them? Do you have something free that you're already giving away and do you have something to sell to their tribe? Make a list of potential JV partners and reach out to that list. Then you want to win them over to have a conversation with you. Then you want to win them over to promote you. Then you want to make sure that your promotion goes really well.

Create your info product with your target market in mind. You need a beginning where you introduce yourself and tell your story. Talk about the challenges. Give an overview of the program, and then jump in and teach all the modules. If you choose, you can include some Q&A at any point before you do a wrap up.

Make special offers. You can sell things through one-on-one sales sessions. You can sell things through presentations—through talks that you would give—through teleclasses, webinars, in person talks, or live stream which is where you would actually do a live video and people can watch all over the Internet.

Here are the three ways to sell things:

1. One-on-one conversations

2. Teleclasses, webinars, and public speaking

3. Sales letters and sales videos

I would recommend if you're going to do some sort of campaign, you could let people buy things from you from all those different ways. You could have a teleclass to launch things off and have a sales video that helps people buy. If people are still not sure, you could potentially even have introductory sessions.

If they don't buy during your promotional phase, then you could offer intro sessions to people who didn't buy, and then potentially sell them coaching with you or sell them your program. You can have a holistic sales approach using all those modalities.

If you want to help people who invest in your program, then use a sales formula. Your sales formula is to talk about the things that they most are looking for. What are the results that they already want? What are the goals they want to achieve? What are the challenges they're facing?

Then tell them about your product and how it's going to help them overcome the challenges they're facing and achieve the results they want, and going into depth in your program and talk about each of those separate particular modules of your training and how those are going to help with certain aspects of their challenges and certain aspects of helping achieve the results they want.

Then you're going to want to tell them the investment, especially having good comparison of what it would cost you if you didn't invest. What else could you invest in—or have you invested in—to help you get these results that probably wouldn't help you as much? Or you could use other types of comparison pricing. Then you'll give the investments they would make with you, potentially having a regular price and a payment plan price.

You also tell them what your guarantee is, if you offer one.

One of the things I teach in "Make Your Programs Make You Millions" is to have a branded guarantee. You want to not only guarantee your products, but you want to make it a guarantee that really stands out, that really makes them feel really compelled to buy your program.

For example, in my "Free Sessions That Sells" program, my branded guarantee is the "Get Clients Guarantee." It's a guarantee that you'll get clients in the first 30 days or you can have a full refund. That's a powerful guarantee. It's a branded guarantee. It's something they're actually going to read and pay attention to. Think about how you can make your guarantee more special if you do decide to offer one and how you can make it more compelling.

That's the formula for selling stuff. Of course if it's a one-on-one sales conversation, then you actually want to ask questions and have people tell you what their goals and challenges are as opposed to telling them what they are.

That's the outline skeleton formula for how to sell something. Then of course there are events that drive sales. Think about what kind of event you could have that would drive the sale.

Product launches are great events to make a lot of sales. Have a "prices going up" event. The price is going to go up, so buy it now before it does. That's a powerful event that drives sales.

A 50% off sale is a great event to drive sales. Adding in special bonuses can be an event—especially if they're limited time bonuses to drive sales.

Or even a certain price point to drive sales. I have a product that I sell for $39 usually, and every now and again we'll do a $7 sale. The reason why we sell it for $7 is certainly it makes us a little bit of money. One time we sold several hundred copies. We may have made $700 or $1400. It's not a huge amount of money, but all of a sudden we're finding people that raise their hand and say, "I'm really interested in the topic," so we could market to those people perhaps a little bit more heavily or offer an introductory coaching session to those people.

There are a lot of different ways you can work all this stuff, and it will be up to you to test things out, or get the help that you need to guide you through the next steps. I hope that now you've got a solid framework for understanding what's involved in creating and selling your info products, and reaching a lot more people with what you have to offer.

CHAPTER 12
The Peace Process

The Peace Process: 7 Simple Steps To Peace In Any Situation

I'm including this powerful process so that on your journey of creating and selling your programs and making a bigger impact in the world, you have a tool to help you get through some of the stuff that will come up for you along the way.

NOTE: Actually follow along with these 7 steps right now as you're reading this, and practice using it whenever something comes up for you.

Step 1: Find the Feeling

All feelings are in your body. Think about the situation that is upsetting you and notice where in your body the feeling is the strongest. Perhaps it will be in your throat, or your chest, or your stomach (these are the most common). But it could be in your hands or your head or anywhere in your body.

Step 2: Give it Attention

Instead of distracting yourself from the feeling, or trying to mentally solve the problem, just be present to the physical sensation of the feeling in your body.

Step 3: Be Unconditionally Loving (or Accepting)

This feeling is here. It's a fact. It won't be here forever (though it might feel that way in the moment). For now, as long as it's here anyway, accept it. And if possible, send that feeling love.

Step 4: Focus on the Eye of Storm

Inside the feeling in your body, there's an area of greatest intensity. Put your attention on it and stay present to it (in an unconditionally loving or accepting way).

Step 5: Let it Breathe

As you give the feeling attention, it may shift in some way. It might get more intense, or less intense. It might move to different parts of your body. Stay with it and let it run its course. It's like an oil candle. The fuel needs oxygen to burn, but once it's burned out it's over. Your attention is the oxygen and the feeling is the fuel. We never know how much fuel is in there.

That's why we never know how long the Peace Process will take. Sometimes seconds. Sometimes minutes. And on very rare occasions, you might need several hours (or separate focused sessions).

Step 6: Get to Peace

Stay with the feeling. Let it live and breathe and grow. Let it move around if it needs to. Keep your attention on the most intense part in an unconditionally loving way. And eventually you'll be at Peace. Again, this will usually happen in 5-10 minutes—sometimes faster, sometimes a bit longer.

Step 7: Permanent Peace

After the feeling has run its course, you'll be left with a neutral feeling. That's peace. You might also be filled with joy or love. That's fun when that happens, but usually it's just sort of a neutral feeling of peace.

To make sure that you've cleared this up completely, think about the situation, problem, or fear that was bothering you. Notice if you feel anything other than peace, love, or joy. If there's anything that isn't peaceful yet, repeat this process over again. Sometimes there are several layers that need to be processed out.

However, in most cases you're now FREE of the FEAR or angst that was keeping you from being at your best.

THIS is the place that you want to make decisions from. This is the place that you want to take action from. This is where you can achieve your highest potential. This is how you have permanent peace around a situation that may have totally owned you in the past.

The Peace Process is a very powerful and valuable way to transform your entire life into something quite magical and to reclaim your greatest self.

I wish you well in your journey as you go forward and create your info products to reach more and more people. And I want you to know that I am here to support you along the way. Feel free to reach out to me at any time.

Your Friend and Coach,

Christian

ABOUT THE AUTHOR

Christian Mickelsen is a leading authority on personal development and personal coaching. He's the author of *How to Quickly Get Started As a Personal Coach: Make Great Money Changing People's Lives*, *Get Clients Today: How To Get A Surge Of New, High Paying Coaching Clients Today And Every Day*, and the upcoming book *The Solution To All Of Life's Problems*.

He's been seen in Forbes, Yahoo Finance, MSN, and the Boston Globe.

He's the founder of IMPACT - the world's leading association for personal coaches

As a personal coach for over 13 years and a trainer of coaches, he's helped countless thousands around the world experience the life changing power of coaching. He's on a mission to get the whole world coached.

He lives in San Diego, California with his wife and two daughters.

Find him here:

http://www.CoachesWithClients.com

http://www.ImpactForCoaches.org

http://www.ChristianMickelsen.com

http://www.facebook.com/christian.mickelsen

http://coacheswithclients.com/twitter

http://coacheswithclients.com/facebook

http://coacheswithclients.com/linkedin

Or contact him at Coaches With Clients:

Christian@CoachesWithClients.com

619-320-8185